I0494621

15 14 13 12 11 10 09 08   8 7 6 5 4 2 2 2

Friends and Gems Acrylic Painting Lesson for Beginners
Dragonfly
Step by step instructions for dragonfly with spatter technique
And Inspirational Story, Poem and Bible Lesson

ISBN-13: 978-1530125401 ISBN-10: 1530125405

By Reverend Bonnie McPhail
angelcare6@yahoo.com
TheFathersMarket@Etsy.com

CreateSpace Independent Publishing Platform

Friends and Gems
Acrylic Painting Lessons for Beginners
Dragonfly

Step by step instructions for Acrylic Butterfly Painting
and inspirational story, poem and bible lesson

By

Reverend Bonnie McPhail

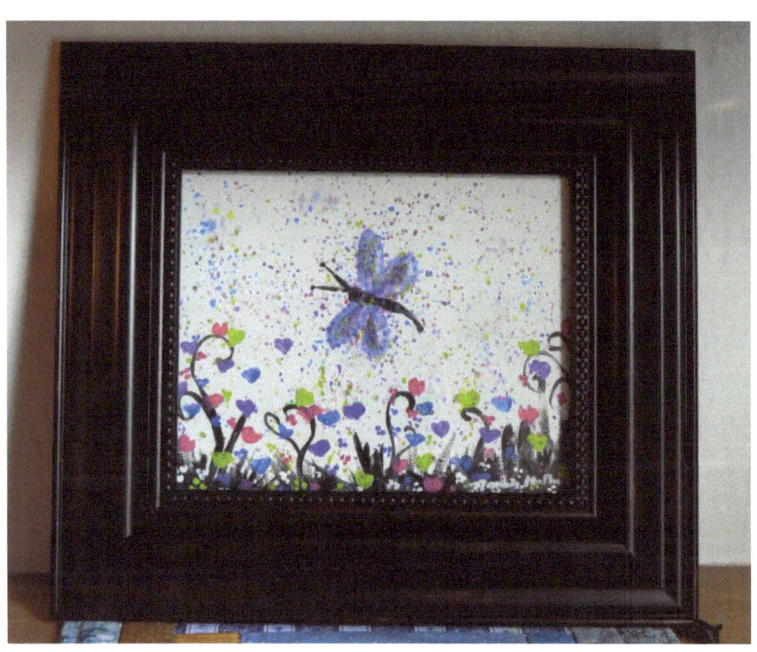

Had an awesome night with Girls Club. We had a guest tonight, Rev. Bonnie McPhail. She is an artist and author. She taught the girls to paint their own ceramic angel, told testimonies to them and also gave autographed books to all the girls which ranged in age from 4-17. There were 17 girls in attendance. They all went home with beautiful angels and joyfulness filled their hearts. They all felt Jesus love. Thank you Bonnie McPhail for everything.
Cindy Bassett National Girls Ministy Milton Assembly of God

Things here at Chandler are going great. Our ladies had lots of positive comments from the service you were with us, you were truly a blessing. Thanks again for your kind words and for thinking of us here at Chandler Assembly

Judy Martin
Pastor's Wife
Chandler First Assembly

My ladies really enjoyed the evening we spent with Bonnie McPhail. Not only did we learn to make elegant candles, soaps and lotions we also learned a little bit about ourselves and each other as we laughed together and enjoyed Bonnies sweet gentle spirit and creative teaching. Bonnie has a true gift for ministry and a way of making every lady feel special.

Jessica Ramirez
Women's Ministry Coordinator
New Life Center

My passion is coaching others to find their sweet spot, the place where their God-given talent and abilities takes flight in their own unique way. When Bonnie began publishing her writings, I was thrilled. Bonnie is an example to other women to rise up and start doing what God has been prompting.

The ideas and crafts will inspire you to grab some girlfriends and create beautiful gifts together, while being encouraged by the uplifting stories. I can sincerely say that everything Bonnie writes is from a heart full of Christ's love. Open your heart to receive these words of love, and be ready to take flight in your unique way!

-Kathy Key, Life Coach & Women's Ministries Leader

Dedicated with love

Savannah Marie McPhail
My beautiful granddaughter and first grandchild,
You are the treasure of my heart,
a longing fulfilled and a prayer answered.
May you use all your gifts of intelligence, beauty,
leadership and kindness to the glory of the Lord.
May you know his love and care of you all the
days of you life and may you know how very
much we all treasure and love you!
~Grammie McPhail~

Horizons of the Promise

Look to the horizon what do you see? There is a new day filled with promise! The past is behind you. Its essence part of the fabric of your experience. A beautiful tapestry, the sum of the parts of your life. Woven by the master to bring growth, strength, and inner wisdom.

It is time to put the past away. There are new horizons, new experiences, and new adventures! Horizons of the promise of good things to come.

Scripture

"and we know that God causes everything to work together for the good of those who love God and are called according to His purposes for them." Romans 8:28 NLT

The Tapestry

By

Reverend Bonnie McPhail

It had been an unbelievably difficult day. I was going through a set of one of the most tumultuous life circumstances I had ever faced.

I was being bombarded at every turn. Not only had my son just returned from a deployment in Iraq, but my business was floundering. I had worked myself into utter exhaustion trying to salvage it, and we were now faced with a long grueling move across country.

Moving was going to mean that my two married children would stay with their own families and the other two who were single at the time would be going with us. My family was getting ready to be split in half.

On top of that my first grandchild was on the way. I had waited years and asked God for this little person and now I was going to miss going through the pregnancy and being there for the precious birth. I was heartbroken.

To say I felt weary, depressed and discouraged was an understatement.

This particular night I had gone to bed exhausted in body, mind and spirit. I didn't have it in myself to even pray and there were no more tears left, I just didn't have the energy.

Sometime in the middle of the night, unable to sleep I decided to get up and read my bible. Perhaps it would quiet the tormenting thoughts I was having.

I sat up on the side of the bed and amazingly I could see this beautiful angelic being. It was HUGE and literally went from one end of the room to the other.

Unbelievable I wasn't fearful or nervous; I just felt this amazingly calm and loving assurance.

The angelic being was dressed in the most beautiful garment I had ever seen in my life. Shades of the earth were all blended into a lovely palette. There was a glittering golden thread interwoven through out that I was immediately drawn to.

In that instant I was given the understanding that our lives are just like the amazing garment I had seen. All of the experiences each had their own color, beautiful in their own right and with their own purpose, fitted together and perfectly combined to make the garment that covers, protects, and is tangible proof of who we are to those around us to see.

I was given the understanding that all the difficulties I was experiencing were part of my garment. In fact, they were the very golden thread that was woven through it.

In the bible gold is often referred to when we have gone through the fire and been refined.

The hardest and most difficult times were the times of refining that brought forth the exquisite beauty of the golden thread, and the strength of that thread is what held it all together and became the most significant color of the garment.

I woke up the next morning with a new excitement in my spirit. Instead of dread I was filled with anticipation. God was getting ready to do something new in my life. There were new horizons up ahead and He had me on an amazing adventure; all I had to do was be willing.

Your life is a tapestry too, interwoven with your own unique and beautiful colors, you have gone through your fire too, but new horizons are up ahead and the promise of good things to come.

Introduction

To my dear sisters and cherished friends,

We as women get so busy! We go to work, take care of our children and husbands, and do all the errands to keep the house running. On and on it goes.

We see our friends at church, in passing, or at the grocery store, and always comment on how we should get together— but then we don't. And we say the same thing the next time we see them. Does this sound familiar?

Friends and Gems Acrylic Painting Lesson for Beginners – Dragonfly is a wonderful combination of spiritual lessons ("gems") and an actual painting lesson. This is the eleventh book in the Friends and Gems series; it is designed to be used by women either in a small-group setting or alone in your own personal quiet time.

The course includes simple step-by-step instructions and to create the beautiful acrylic painting featured on the cover. Step by step photographs are included.

I wanted to make this not only a painting tutorial but a relaxing time of peace and inner reflection. So I have included stories, poetry, simple bible lessons, scriptures and places for you to record your thoughts while you work on your project either alone or in a group.

Along the way, you will learn life changing spiritual truths that you can apply to your own life, all while spending time with your friends.

Sound like fun? Let's get started!

Materials

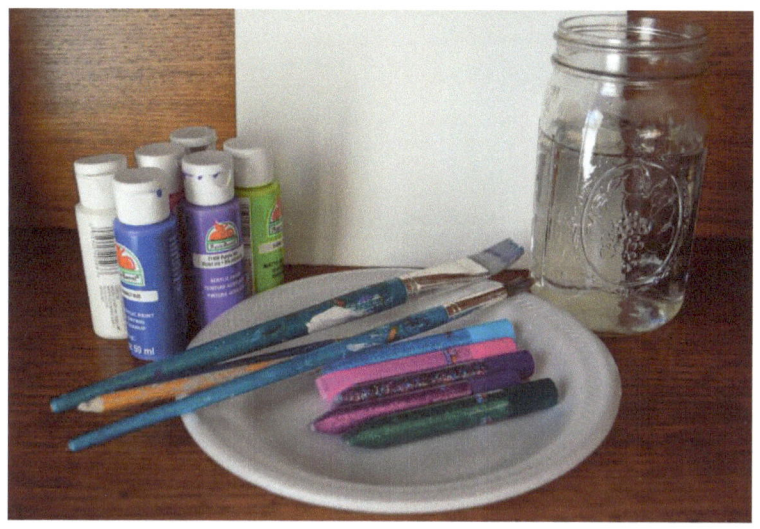

For this project you will need a jar of water, 8x10 stretched canvas, all the colors of the rainbows acrylic paints, a small plastic spatula, flat brush, round brush and sponge.

Step One

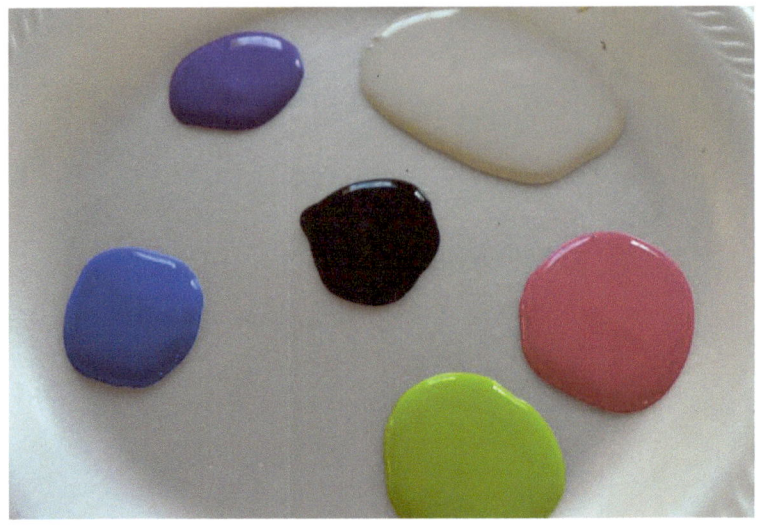

Squeeze a small amount of all the paint colors
onto a paper plate.

Step Two

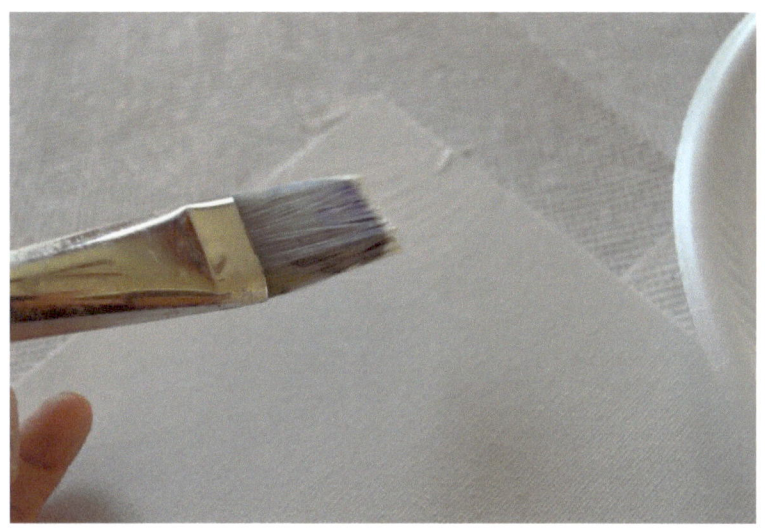

Start with the white paint and cover the canvas

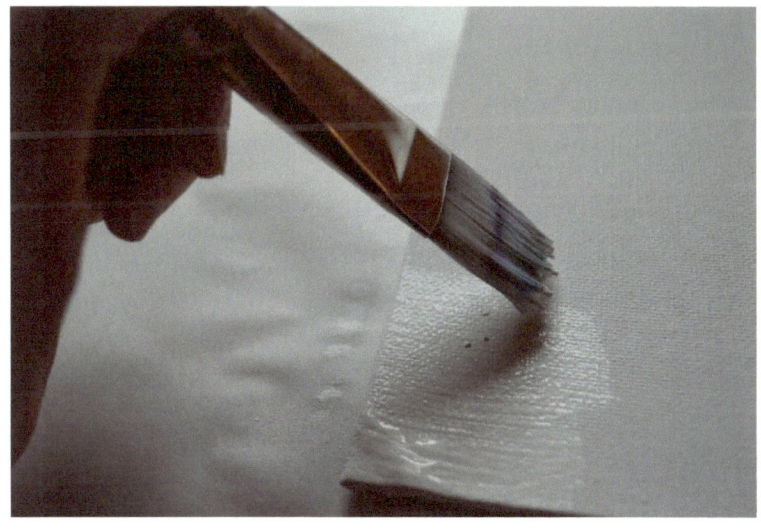

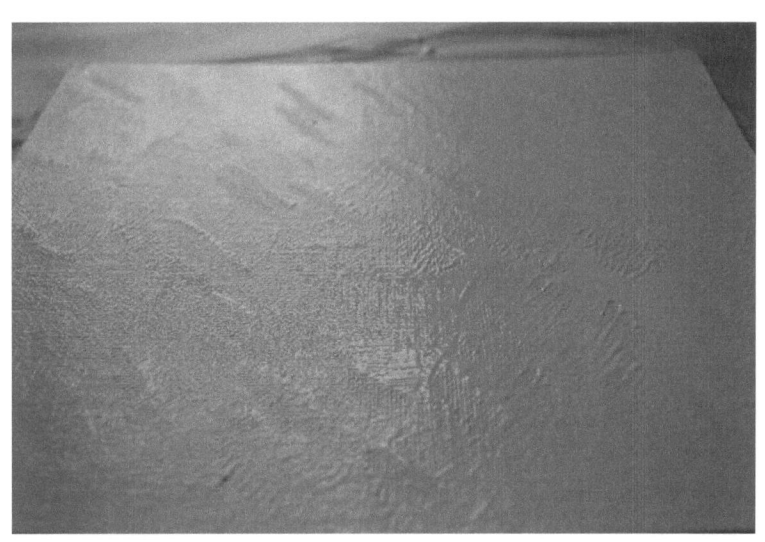

You will want to cover the entire surface of the canvas. You can leave any texture you want it will add to the nice dimension later.

Step Three

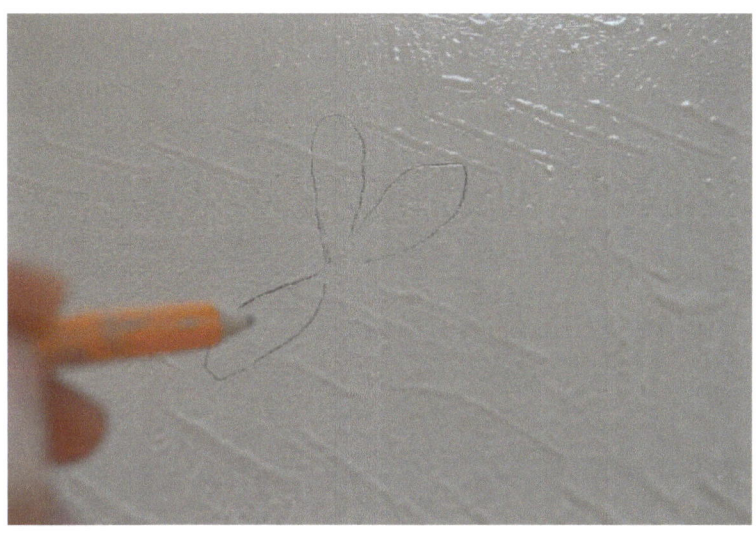

Using a pencil lightly sketch the outline of the dragonfly

Step Four

Step Five

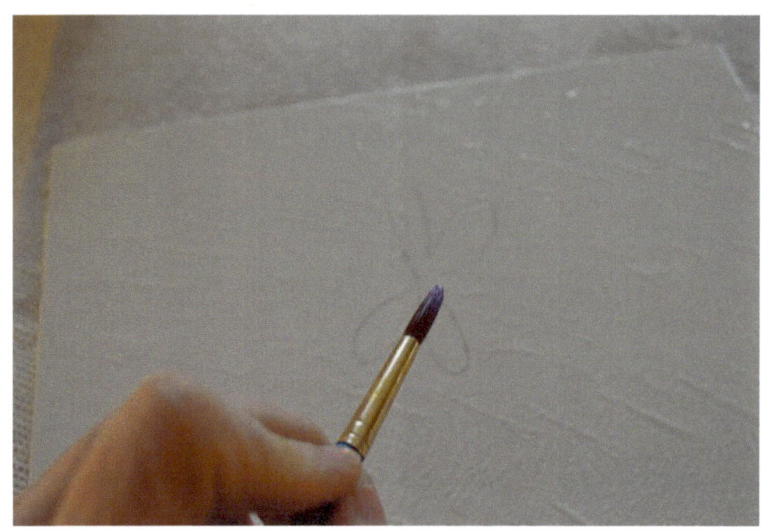

We will be creating a beautiful "spatter" pattern all over the surface of the canvas. Start out by choosing a light color first and water it down so it will spatter easily.

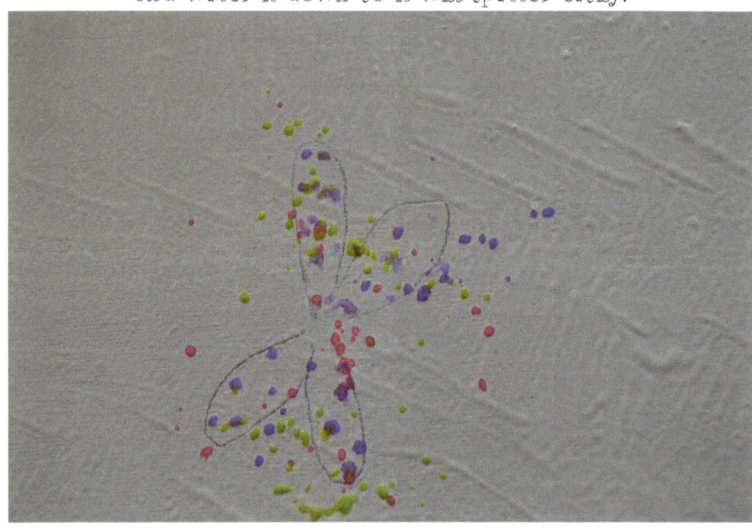

Step Six

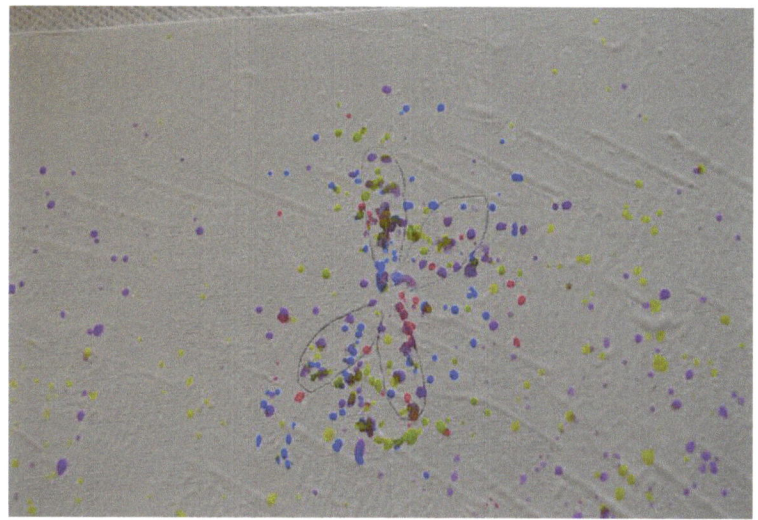

Using two paintbrushes tap one with the other. The paint will spatter. You will want to hold the brush close to the page.

Step Seven

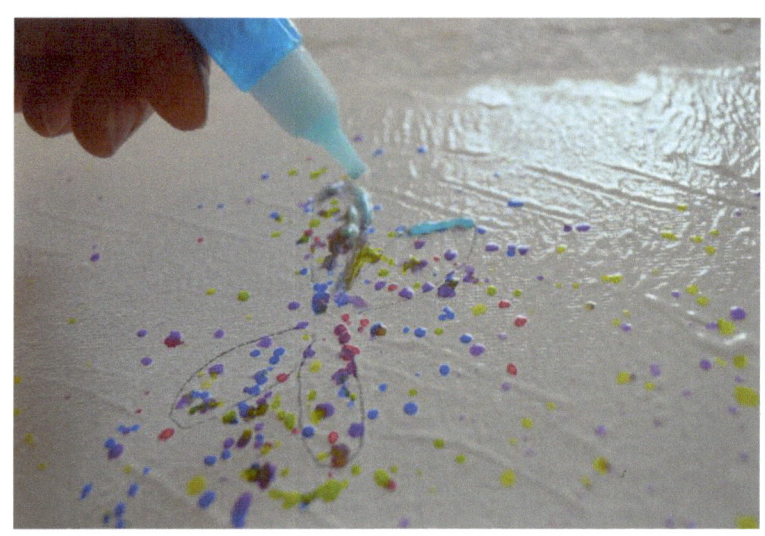

Next outline the dragonfly with glitter glue

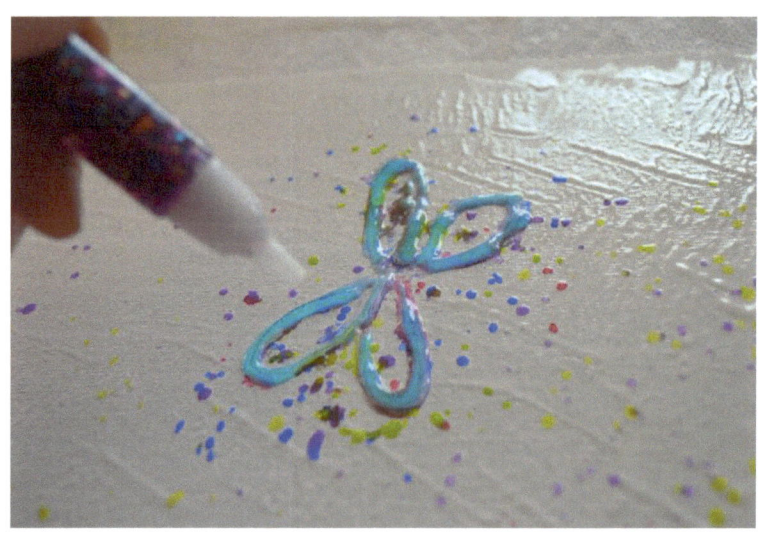

Step Eight

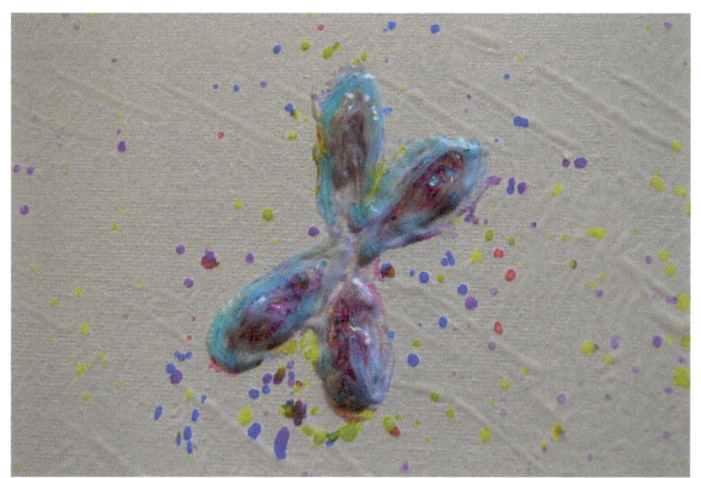

Fill in the wings with the purple glitter glue

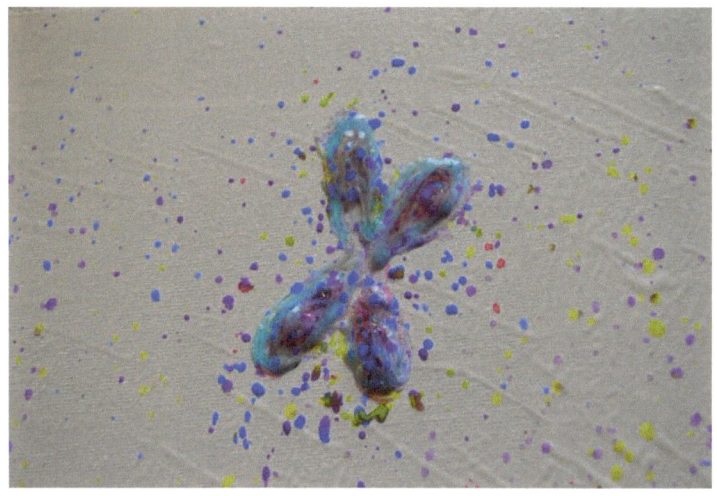

Spatter more paint over the glitter glue wings

Step Nine

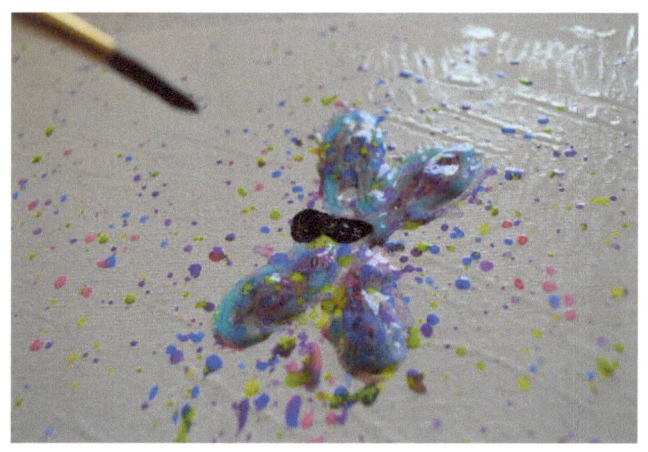

Paint the head and body of the dragonfly with black paint

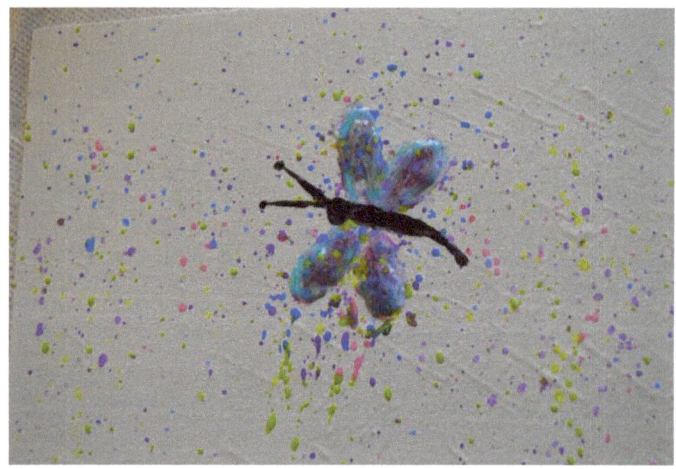

Add the antennae

Step Ten

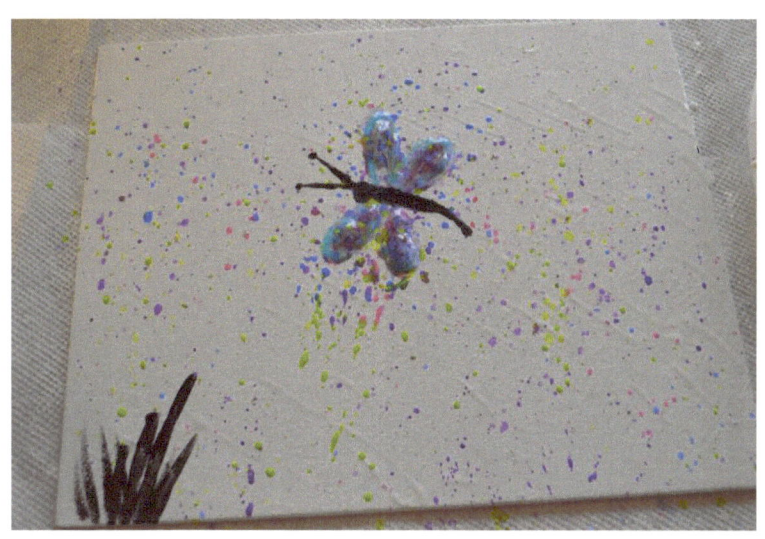

Start adding the grass across the bottom with black paint

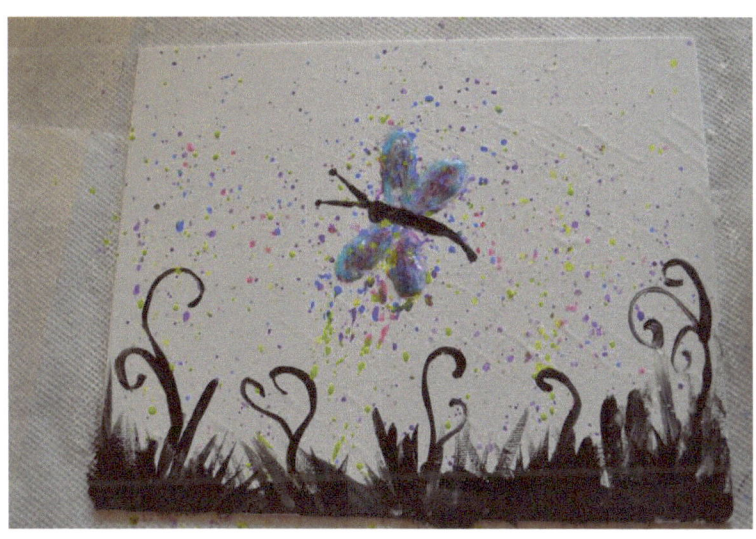

Step Eleven

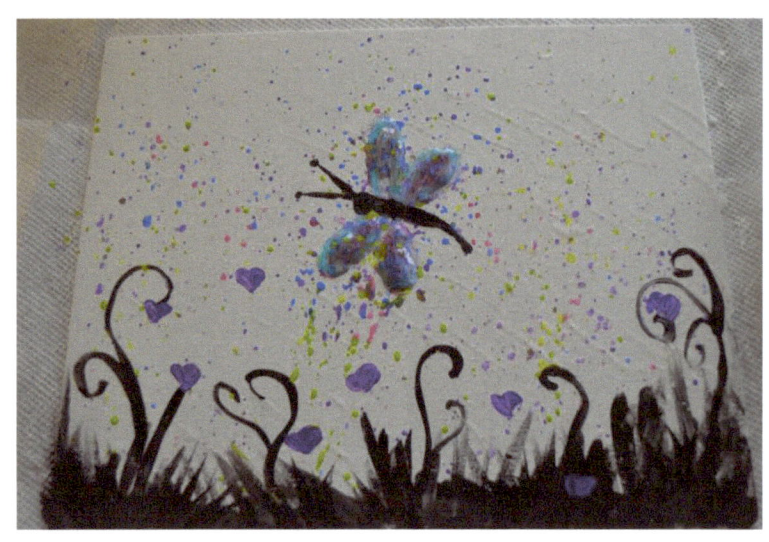

Paint the hearts

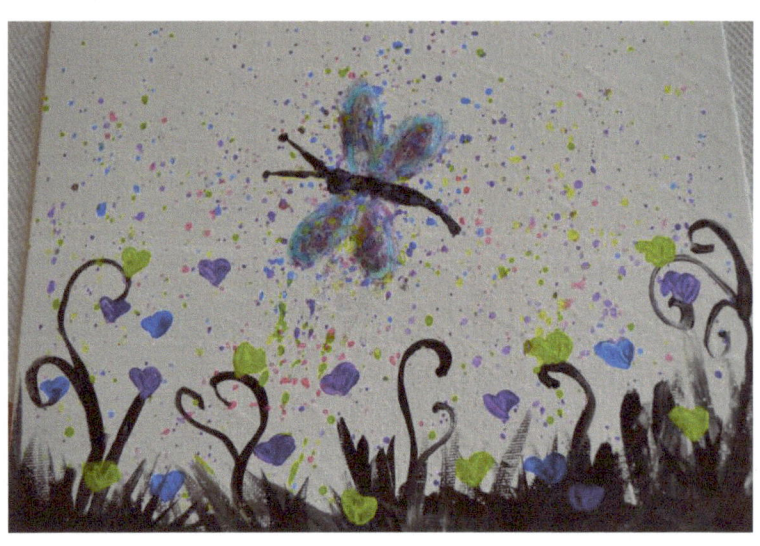

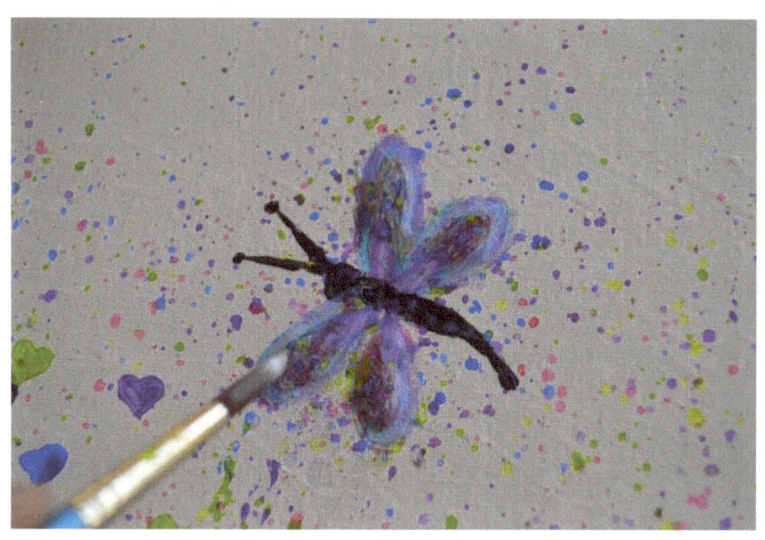

Add purple and blue around the edges of the wings

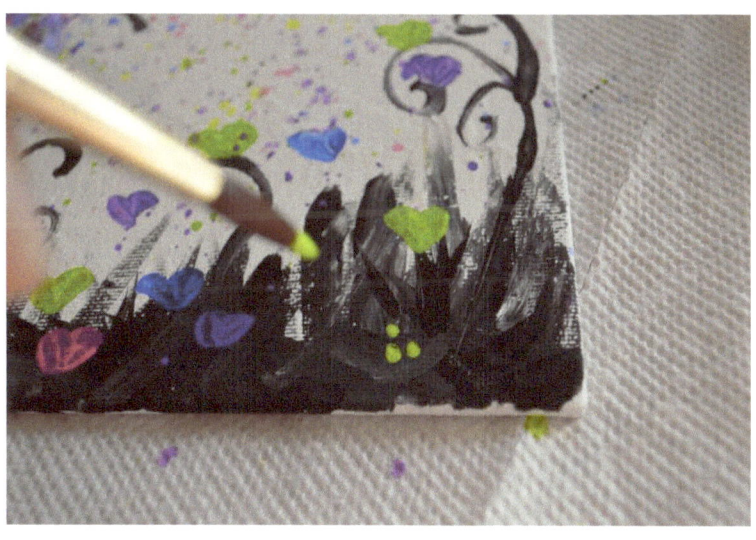

Dipt the brush in paint and make three dots

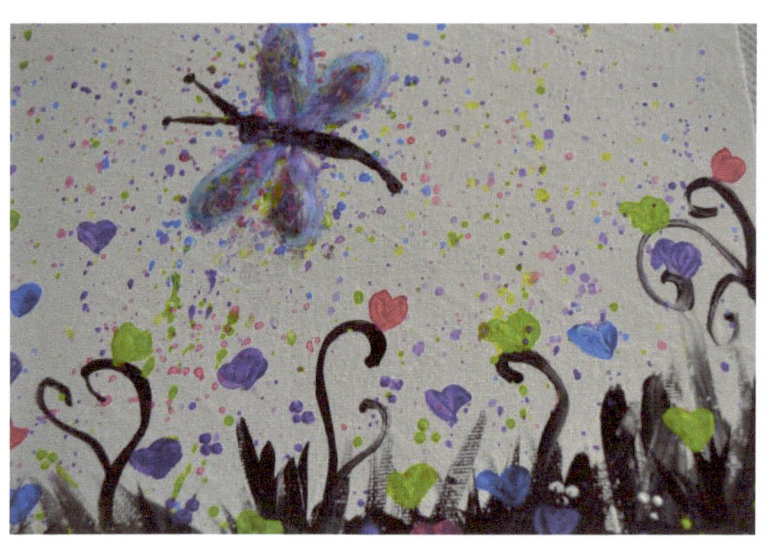

More spatters and more hearts

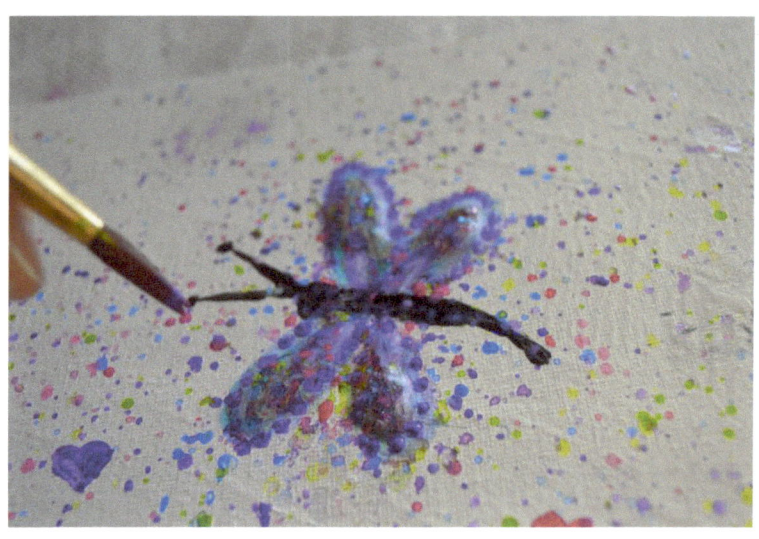

Step Twelve

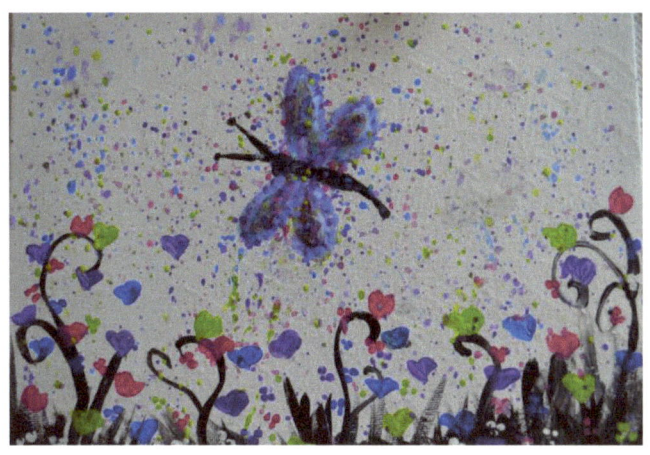

Dip the brush in the blue paint and make tiny dots all the way around the outline of the dragonfly wings

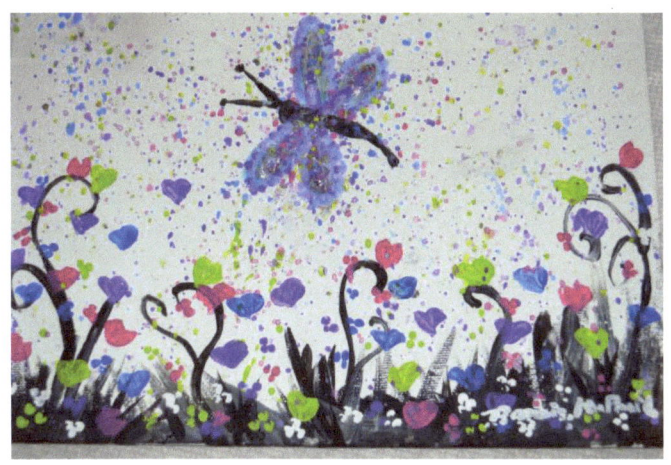

Don't forget to sign your name!

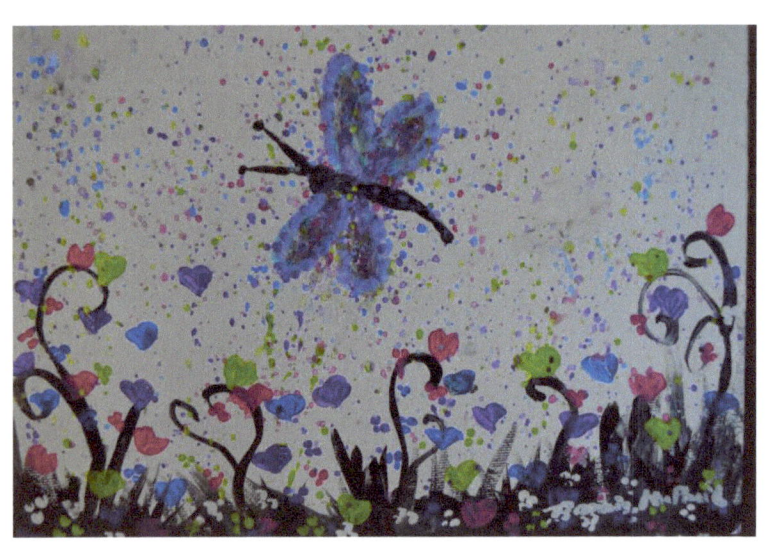

Step Thirteen

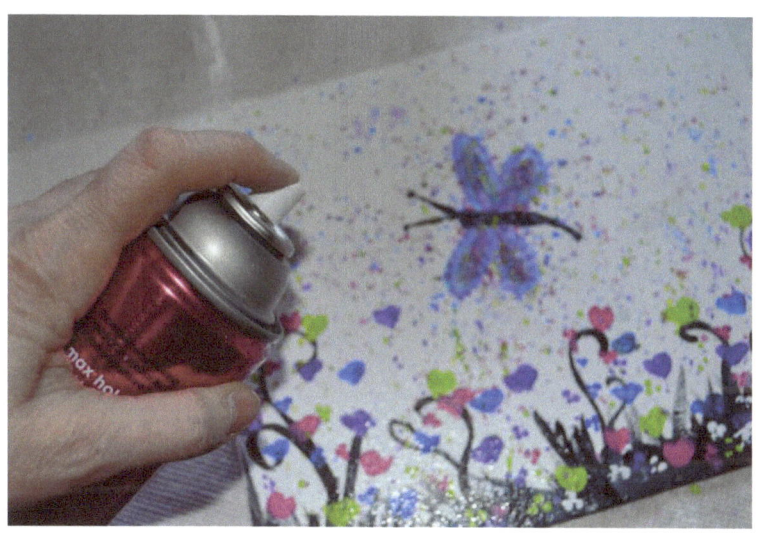

Spray with hairspray. This will seal your painting. Set it aside
to dry and now we will work on the bible study.

Bible Lesson
All Things Work Together for Good

Did you know that all things really do work together for your good? Have you ever wondered how this can possible happen when circumstances seem so impossible?

We are going to be taking this familiar scripture verse and breaking it down using the Greek meanings. All of the greek words can be referenced in *Strong's Exhaustive Concordance of the Bible* by James Strong.

For future references we will be using Strong's for any Greek words.

The words underlined in the passage taken from the King James version of the bible are the words we will be searching for the deeper meaning in the Greek.

"We know that all things <u>work</u> together for <u>good</u> to them that <u>love</u> God, to them who are <u>called</u> according to his <u>purpose</u>." Romans 8:28 KJV

Work – Greek – Sunergeo – to be a fellow worker, cooperate, work together.

Good – Greek – Agathos – benefit.

Love – Greek – Fileo – to be a friend to.

Called – Greek – Kletos – from the same as, invited, appointed.

Purpose- Greek – Prothesis – a setting forth (shew bread), proposal, intentional.

Let's take a look at the word work in this verse; we see that "all things" which means everything in our lives, the good as well as the bad, we are not alone; Jesus is a fellow worker TOGETHER WITH US.

1. Can you think of a situation in your life where you saw that the Lord was working with you?

_____
_____
_____
_____
_____
_____
_____
_____
_____
_____
_____
_____

2. What was the end result?

_____
_____
_____
_____
_____
_____
_____
_____
_____
_____
_____
_____
_____
_____
_____

Next let's look at the word good: which means
benefit. We see the Lord is working together with
us FOR OUR BENEFIT.

3. Can you think of a situation that worked out for
your benefit?

_____
_____
_____
_____
_____
_____
_____
_____
_____
_____

The next word in our list is love: To be a friend
to. The greek work is Fileos which is human love.
So this means that God wants us even in our
humanity to love him like he is our friend. WOW
the creator of the universe whats us to be his friend!

4. What is your best friends attributes:

_____
_____
_____
_____
_____
_____
_____
_____
_____
_____

5. List the ways in which you can be God's friend.

_____
_____
_____
_____
_____
_____
_____
_____
_____
_____

The next word on our list: called means to be invited or appointed. God invites us to a personal relationship as his friend through his son Jesus. This word is significant because it is not forced. In other words God does not force us to know him. He gently invites us. The choice belongs to us.

If you would like to accept this gift from God please repeat this prayer:

Dear Jesus,

I ask you to come into my heart and forgive me. I believe you are the son of God that you are Lord and that you died on a cross for me. I accept the free gift of your friendship now.

Once you say that prayer the bible says you now can be a friend of God, an actual child of His, with all the love and benefits. Angels are rejoicing in heaven because now you have your name written in the book of life and you will go to heaven after you die. Your life will never be the same!

The last word on the list is purpose which in the Greek is setting forth, proposal, intentional, show bread.

In the old testament shew bread was made from flour and oil and it was the bread that was used in the temple. It represents God's covenant with us. It was to be put before his face every Sabbath as a continual reminder of his covenant with his children. "and every Sabbath he shall set it in order before the Lord continually being taken from the children of Israel to an everlasting covenant." Leviticus 24:8 NKJV.

The same scripture is referenced in the New Testament in John 6:48 KJV (Jesus speaking) "I am the bread of life."

Jesus is the shew bread, the covenant continually before God's face for us. To paraphrase the verse we have been studying into a very simple format by taking the Greek words and inserting them, the verse would mean something like this: Everything will be for our benefit, to we who are invited to be God's friends because Jesus is working together with us. He makes it possible for all things towork out for good because He is the covenant standing in our place before God continually.

All Framed and Ready to Go!

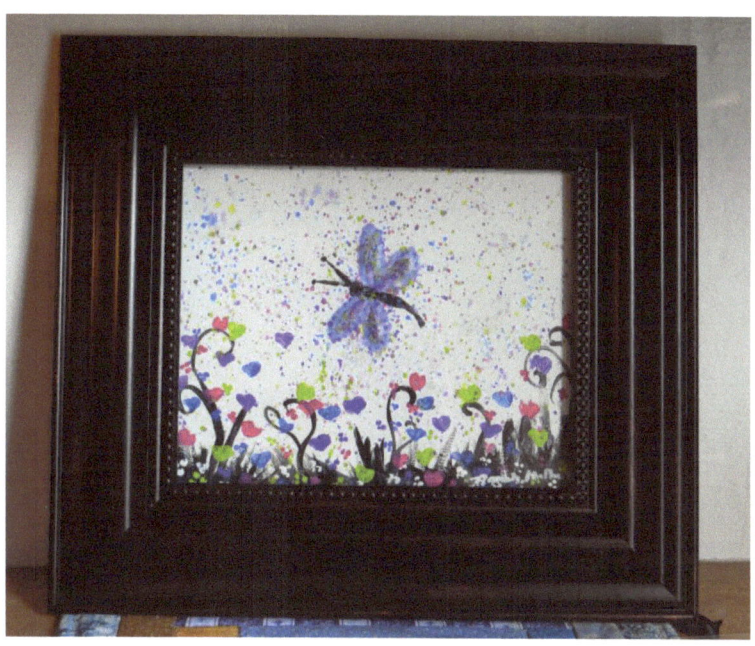

This would be such a fun project to do with your
children and grandchildren as well as your friends.

Good Comes

"I will take the most difficult seasons of your life and turn them around for your good. My heart beats for you to know the depth of my love for you. Great good shall be accomplished, trust me in this. I am true to my word. I have not forsaken or abandoned you. I will not leave you."

~The Lord~

Scripture

"and we know that all things work together for good to those who love God, to those who are called according to his purpose." Romans 8:28 NKJV

About the Author

Reverend Bonnie McPhail has a B.S. in Organizational Management and Ethics, an A.S.N. in Nursing, and certifications both in pastoral studies and life coaching. She is an ordained Assembly of God minister. Her nursing background gives her special insight into the emotional and physical needs of women, and she serves as a pastor to women when she ministers to them. Her work has been published both nationally and internationally, and she is available for conferences and workshops.

You can contact her via email if you would like to schedule a class or workshop at angelcare6@yahoo.com

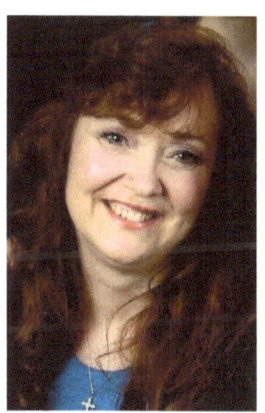

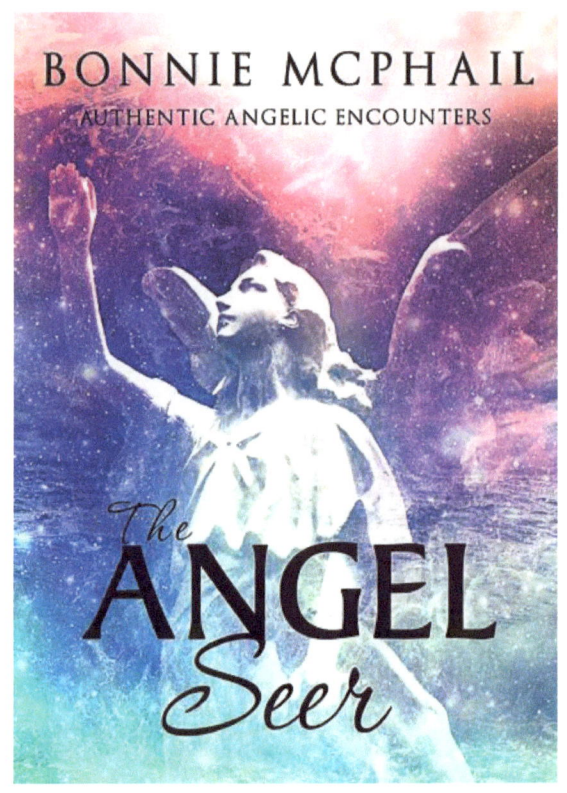

BONNIE MCPHAIL
AUTHENTIC ANGELIC ENCOUNTERS

The
ANGEL
Seer

Available on Amazon, Winters Publishing Group and
TheFathersMarket@Etsy.com

Most people believe in angels but have never seen them. The Angel Seer describes actual angelic encounters experienced by the author along with her supernatural experiences, which will show you how you are personally and individually loved and taken care of. You will learn for yourself how to recognize them when they are personally involved in your own life.

Bonnie McPhail has a remarkable ability to see into the spiritual realm with child-like faith; yet, she remains grounded in the here and now reality of life on earth.

The Angel Seer is Bonnie McPhail's own journey in which we see the ripple effect in the kingdom of God. Each and every manifestation of the Holy Spirit changes us so we can no longer live an ordinary life. Whether we find ourselves in the valley of difficult beginnings or the mountain of angelic encounters, there is work being done in both the physical and spiritual realms accomplishing all God has planned.

Rev. Ann Callahan, M.A.M.L.
Pastoral Care Coach/Chaplain

As a child growing up in a Pentecostal church, supernatural physical manifestations from the Lord were expected. Miraculous healings and divine interventions confirmed the real and tangible work in the unseen spiritual world. Yet no one I knew ever said they saw an angel, until I met Bonnie.

To actually see an angel must be frightening, yet awe-inspiring. Bonnie has experienced what most people do not see -- the unseen spiritual world. Her stories inspire the physical eye to look beyond the tangible and glimpse the glory beyond. Her prayer as a child that God would make Himself real to her has been answered in ways her childlike heart never imagined. His divine work gloriously confirms to all who read these pages that He is present, whether we see or not.

As you read the angelic encounters Bonnie has experienced, you may think this woman is a bit strange, perhaps off her rocker. I can assure you she is not. Bonnie is the most real, down to earth woman you could ever meet. She's witty, fun, strong, loving and kind. She is the woman you want to have heartwarming talks with over a cup of coffee. She is ever the encourager, building people up to find hope in divine possibilities.

Bonnie's stories will stir your heart to a heavenly awareness that the Lord is with you and His angels are all around. Her book encourages the reader to hope for what is not seen, putting faith in the powerful, Almighty God. Bonnie's stories are written for your benefit, to testify and to confirm the truth that yes, God is real and His angels are working as He commands!

-Rev. Kathy Key, MACM

Executive Director, Love is the Key Ministries, Inc.

It has been my privilege and honor to have known Mrs. Bonnie McPhail for almost twenty years. She has always been an inspiration for me in every way! She has a very strong anointing on her to encourage the body of Christ (all of the books that she has written up to now are very uplifting). The Angel seer, will equip the body of Christ with the tools to understand the spiritual realm of God on a level that has surpassed anything I've ever read. The reading is easy to understand and filled with scripture to back up every experience. I am very excited about this book, I know God has anointed Bonnie to write "The Angel Seer" to be used mightily for the kingdom of God.

Jacqueline Stone

Bonnie and I have known one another for more years than many of you, as readers of this wonderful book, have been alive! We grew up together in rural New Hampshire and became fast friends in 7th Grade. We did absolutely everything together. But in 10th Grade, Bonnie suddenly changed. She started carrying a Bible to school, praying over her meals, and constantly speaking to me about Jesus. We began to grow apart. It wasn't that I didn't believe in God and Jesus, it was just that I certainly didn't need them at the forefront of my life; they were just there for emergencies, right? I soon learned I was very wrong. Through a course of upsetting events in my own life, one Friday night, I reluctantly agreed to go to a youth event with Bonnie, put on by her church; not because I wanted to go, but honestly only because I needed to get out of my house and it was the only place I could go. But it was that night I asked Jesus into my heart...and so began an incredible life-long journey, thanks to Bonnie! Bonnie's undying faith in Jesus and her love for me changed my life forever. No one could have a truer friend. Bonnie has continued, over these many years, to inspire and encourage me. She has a child-like faith in Jesus, eager always to please and honor Him no manner what others around her might think. She is a woman filled with compassion for others, and a deep desire that all would know Jesus as their best friend.

Mona Tardif

We live in difficult days! So many people think things written in the Bible no longer apply today. Yet, the fact remains that the same God that worked in people's lives in the Old and New Testament era of the Bible had genuine spiritual experiences that defied logical explanations. Many people don't realize today that God has an army of messengers or angels that are dispatched to help the saints of God, whether you ever actually see one or not is not the central point, the fact that they are watching over our lives and ministering to us is real. God is still in the business of guiding, helping, watching over, and ministering to His people. The realm of the supernatural is just as real as the world you see and experience every day.

Rev. Dennis Marquardt Superintendent NNED

More Friends and Gems Painting Lessons for Beginners

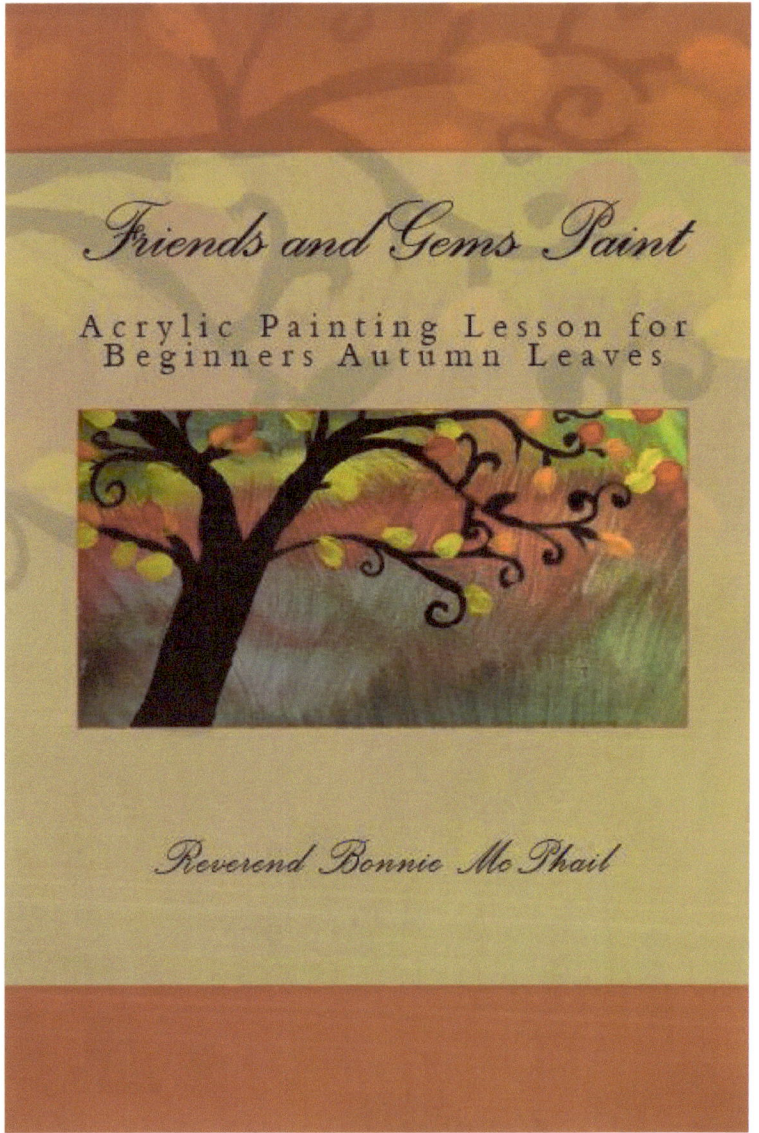

Friends and Gems Paint Acrylic Painting Lesson for Beginners

Step By Step Instructions for Spring Leaves

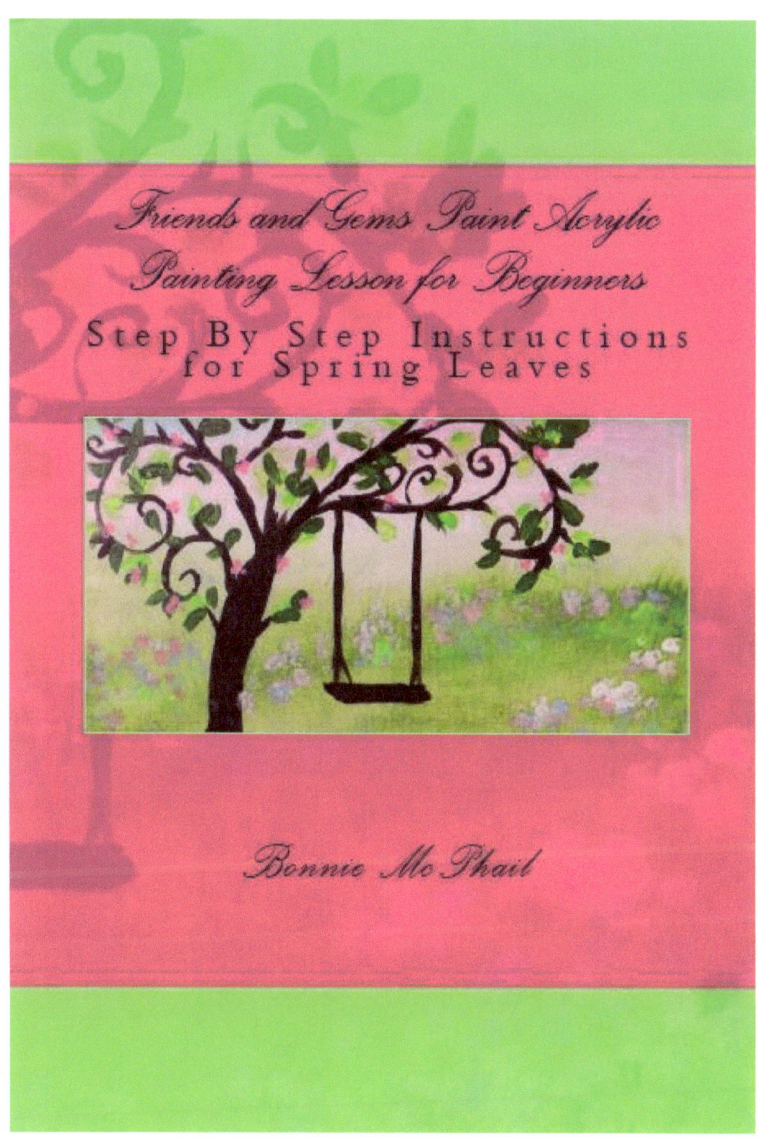

Bonnie Mc Phail

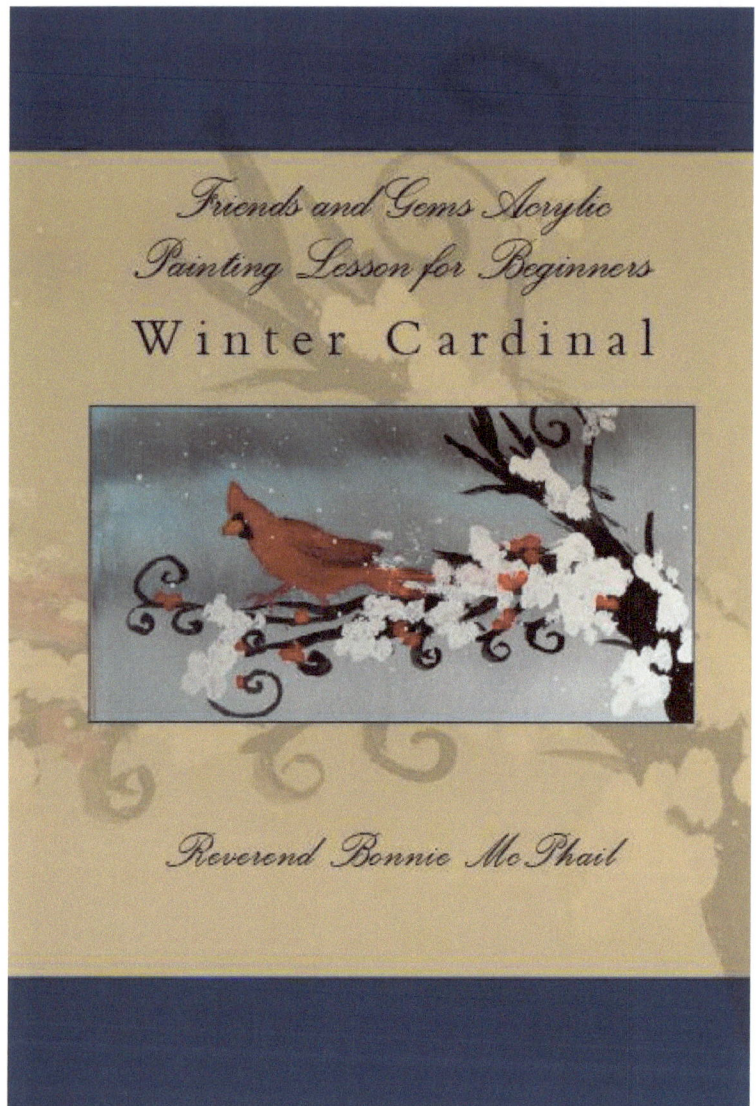

Friends and Gems Acrylic
Painting Lesson for Beginners

Winter Cardinal

Reverend Bonnie McPhail

Friends and Gems
Acrylic Painting Lesson for Beginners

Rainbow Trees

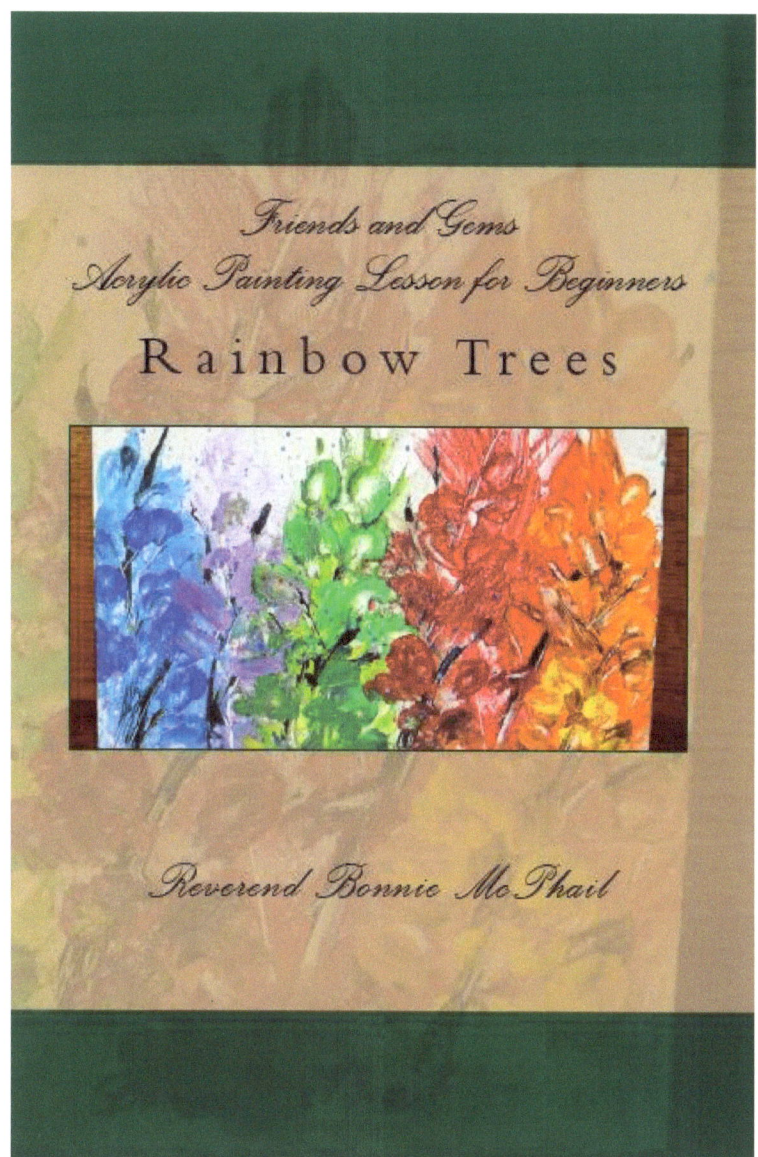

Reverend Bonnie McPhail

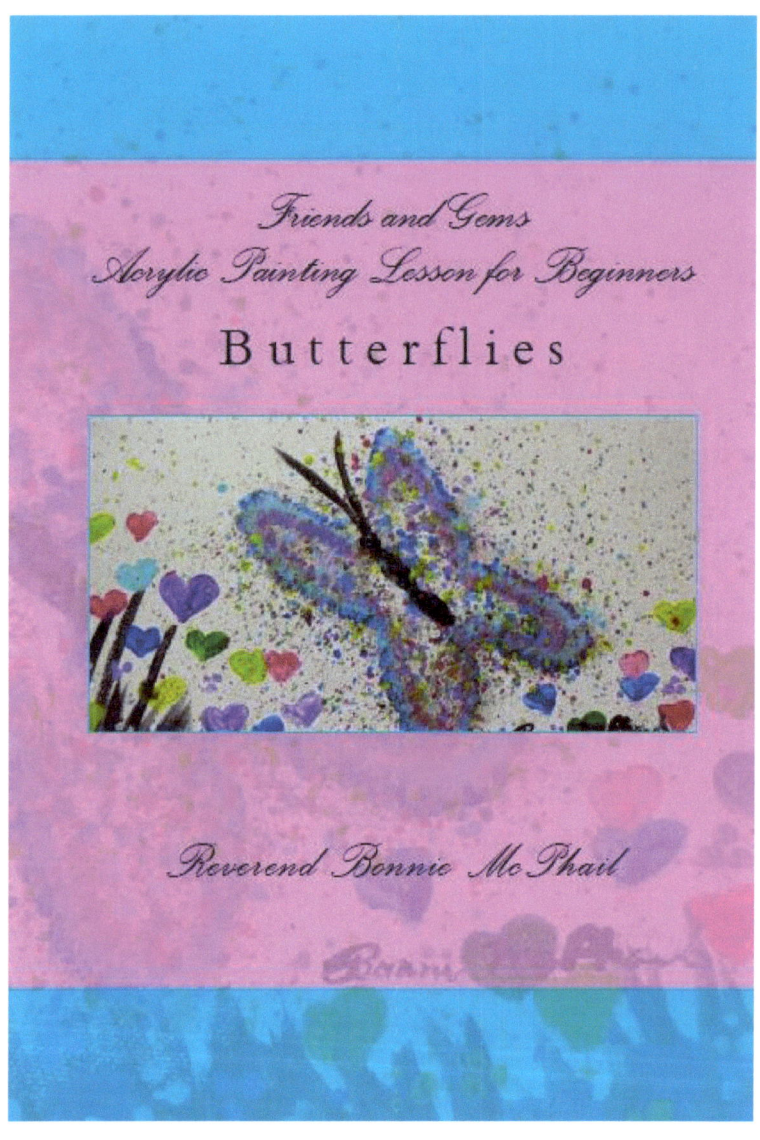

If you are interested in viewing and purchasing more of the authors books and art her work is available at:

TheFathersMarket@Etsy.com

Or on Amazon.

www.ingramcontent.com/pod-product-compliance
Lightning Source LLC
Chambersburg PA
CBHW040924180526
45159CB00002BA/603